As It Is in HEAVEN

A COLLECTION OF PRAYERS FOR ALL AGES

illustrated by
ÉRIC PUYBARET

Éric Puybaret has illustrated over twenty books for children, including *Suite for Human Nature* (Atheneum), *Manfish: A Story of Jacques Cousteau* (Chronicle), and *Puff the Magic Dragon* (Sterling). His work for *As It Is in Heaven*—and many other titles—was inspired by early Italian Renaissance painting. Éric is a graduate of the National School of Decorative Arts in Paris. He lives in France. Visit his website at ericpuybaret.com.

First published in the United States in 2020
by Eerdmans Books for Young Readers,
an imprint of Wm. B. Eerdmans Publishing Co.
Grand Rapids, Michigan

www.eerdmans.com/youngreaders

Originally published in France in 2017 under the title *Prières*
by Mame Éditions, Paris, France
French edition © 2017 Mame Éditions

English-language edition © 2020 Eerdmans Books for Young Readers

Manufactured in China

28 27 26 25 24 23 22 21 20   1 2 3 4 5 6 7 8 9

ISBN 978-0-8028-5538-1

A catalog record of this book is available from the Library of Congress

As It Is in HEAVEN

A COLLECTION OF PRAYERS FOR ALL AGES

illustrated by
ÉRIC PUYBARET

Our Father

Our Father in heaven,
hallowed be your name,
your kingdom come,
your will be done,
on earth as in heaven.
Give us today our daily bread.
Forgive us our sins
as we forgive those who sin against us.
Do not let us fall into temptation
and deliver us from evil.

Amen.

Hail Mary

Hail Mary, full of grace,
the Lord is with you;
blessed are you among women,
and blessed is the fruit of your womb, Jesus.

Holy Mary, Mother of God,
pray for us sinners
now and at the hour of our death.

Amen.

The Apostles' Creed

I believe in God, the Father almighty,
creator of heaven and earth.

I believe in Jesus Christ, God's only Son, our Lord,
who was conceived by the Holy Spirit,
born of the Virgin Mary,
suffered under Pontius Pilate,
was crucified, died, and was buried;
he descended to the dead.
On the third day he rose again;
he ascended into heaven,
he is seated at the right hand of the Father,
and he will come to judge the living and the dead.

I believe in the Holy Spirit,
the holy catholic Church,
the communion of saints,
the forgiveness of sins,
the resurrection of the body,
and the life everlasting.

Amen.

Gloria

Glory to God in the highest,
and on earth peace to people of good will.

We praise you,
we bless you,
we adore you,
we glorify you,
we give you thanks for your great glory,
Lord God, heavenly King,
O God, almighty Father.

Lord Jesus Christ, Only Begotten Son,
Lord God, Lamb of God, Son of the Father,
you take away the sins of the world,
have mercy on us;
you take away the sins of the world,
receive our prayer;
you are seated at the right hand of the Father,
have mercy on us.

For you alone are the Holy One,
you alone are the Lord,
you alone are the Most High,
Jesus Christ,
with the Holy Spirit,
in the glory of God the Father.

Amen.

Morning Prayer

Lord,
in the silence of this new day,
I come to ask for peace, wisdom, and strength.

Today, I wish to look at the world
with eyes beaming with love.
To be understanding, meek, and wise.
To see your children beyond appearances
as You see them yourself.

Close my ears to all calumny.
Guard my tongue from all malice.
May only thoughts that bless
dwell in my spirit.
May I be so kind and so full of joy,
that all who come near me may feel your presence.

Clothe me with your beauty, Lord,
that throughout this day I may reveal You.

Amen.

Veni
Sancte Spiritus

Come, Holy Spirit;
send down from heaven's height
your radiant light.

Come, lamp of every heart,
come, parent of the poor;
all gifts are yours.

Comforter beyond all comforting,
sweet unexpected guest,
sweetly refresh.

Rest in hard labor,
coolness in heavy heat,
hurt souls' relief.

Refill the secret hearts
of your faithful,
O most blessed light.

Without your holy power
nothing can bear your light,
nothing is free from sin.

Wash all that is filthy,
water all that is parched,
heal what is hurt within.

Bend all that is rigid,
warm all that has frozen hard,
lead back the lost.

Give to your faithful ones,
who come in simple trust,
your sevenfold mystery.

Give virtue its reward,
give, in the end, salvation
and joy that has no end.

Amen.

Magnificat

My soul proclaims the greatness of the Lord,
my spirit rejoices in God my Savior,
for you, Lord, have looked with favor on your lowly servant.

From this day all generations will call me blessed:
you, the Almighty, have done great things for me
and holy is your name.

You have mercy on those who fear you,
from generation to generation.

You have shown strength with your arm
and scattered the proud in their conceit,
casting down the mighty from their thrones,
and lifting up the lowly.

You have filled the hungry with good things
and sent the rich away empty.

You have come to the aid of your servant Israel,
to remember the promise of mercy,
the promise made to our forebears,
to Abraham and his children for ever.

Amen.

Prayer for Peace

Lord, make me an instrument of your peace.

Where there is hatred, let me sow love;
where there is injury, pardon;
where there is doubt, faith;
where there is despair, hope;
where there is darkness, light;
and where there is sadness, joy.

O Divine Master, grant that I may not so much seek
to be consoled as to console;
to be understood as to understand;
to be loved as to love.

For it is in giving that we receive;
it is in pardoning that we are pardoned;
and it is in dying that we are born to eternal life.

Amen.

Prayer attributed to Saint Francis of Assisi

Prayer of Abandonment

Father,
I abandon myself into your hands;
do with me what you will.
Whatever you may do, I thank you:
I am ready for all, I accept all.

Let only your will be done in me,
and in all your creatures—
I wish no more than this, O Lord.

Into your hands I commend my soul:
I offer it to you
with all the love of my heart,
for I love you, Lord,
and so need to give myself,
to surrender myself into your hands
without reserve,
and with boundless confidence,
for you are my Father.

Amen.

Prayer by Blessed Charles de Foucauld

The Song of Simeon

Now, Lord, you let your servant go in peace:
your word has been fulfilled.

My own eyes have seen the salvation
which you have prepared in the sight of every people:

a light to reveal you to the nations
and the glory of your people Israel.

Amen.

Lord Jesus,
Teach Us

Lord,
teach me to be generous.
Teach me to serve you as you deserve;
to give and not to count the cost;
to fight and not to heed the wounds;
to toil and not to seek for rest;
to labor and not to ask for reward
save that of knowing
that I do your will.

Amen.

Prayer attributed to Saint Ignatius Loyola

Breathe in Me, O Holy Spirit

Breathe in me, O Holy Spirit,
that my thoughts may all be holy.

Act in me, O Holy Spirit,
that my work, too, may be holy.

Draw my heart, O Holy Spirit,
that I love but what is holy.

Strengthen me, O Holy Spirit,
to defend all that is holy.

Guard me, then, O Holy Spirit,
that I always may be holy.

Amen.

Prayer attributed to Saint Augustine

Memorare

Remember, O most gracious Virgin Mary,
that never was it known
that anyone who fled to your protection,
implored your help,
or sought your intercession was left unaided.

Inspired by this confidence,
we fly unto you,
O Virgin of virgins,
our mother.
To you we come,
before you we stand,
sinful and sorrowful.
O Mother of the Word Incarnate,
despise not our petitions,
but in your mercy hear and answer us.

Amen.

Glorious
Saint Joseph

Glorious Saint Joseph, spouse of Mary,
grant us your paternal protection,
we beseech you by the heart of Jesus Christ.

O Saint Joseph,
whose power extends to all our necessities
and can render possible for us the most impossible things,
open your fatherly eyes to the needs of your children.

Amen.

Prayer attributed to Saint Francis de Sales

Sources

English translations of
"Apostles' Creed," "Magnificat," "Our Father," "Song of Simeon"
© 1988 English Language Liturgical Consultation (ELLC)
www.englishtexts.org
Used by permission.

"Breathe in Me, O Holy Spirit"
courtesy Villanova University,
villanova.edu/mission/campusministry

"Gloria" from *The Roman Missal*
©2010 International Commission on English in the Liturgy Corporation (ICEL)
All rights reserved

"Glorious St. Joseph"
courtesy Shrine of Christ the King Sovereign Priest,
https://www.shrinelandmark.org/wp-content/uploads/2017/12/St-Joseph-March-Prayer.pdf

"Hail Mary"
courtesy United States Conference of Catholic Bishops,
usccb.org/prayerandworship.

"Lord Jesus, Teach Us" and "Memorare"
courtesy Marquette University,
marquette.edu/faith/prayers-traditional.php

"Morning Prayer"
courtesy Sisters of Saint Joseph of Saint-Hyacinthe,
sjsh.org/43-pray-morning-prayer.html

"Prayer for Peace"
courtesy Franciscan Media,
info.franciscanmedia.org/catholic-prayers

"Prayer of Abandonment"
courtesy North American Jesus Caritas Communities,
brothercharles.org/wordpress

"Veni Sancte Spiritus"
courtesy Church of England,
churchofengland.org/prayer-and-worship